The Top Recruit

A Student-Athlete's Guide to Being Recruited

Anthony Drew Harrison

ISBN-13:
978-1544822228

ISBN-10:
1544822227

Cover design and photography by James Kintu
Editing by Dr. Henry Roubicek & Stephanie Schottel

ABOUT THE AUTHOR

Once going through the recruiting process himself as one of Houston's top football recruits and athletes, Anthony Harrison decided to assist families with their student-athlete's recruiting process. Anthony received letters and phone calls from the top universities in America including: LSU, Miami, Notre Dame, Cal Berkeley, Northwestern, Brown, Columbia and Texas A&M to name a few. Using the methods in the book Anthony decided to accept a full scholarship to Louisiana Tech University home of legends such as: Terry Bradshaw, Karl Malone, Willie Roaf, Teresa Weatherspoon and the owners of Duck Dynasty to mention a few. Anthony chose Louisiana Tech over TCU, Baylor, Oklahoma State and Air Force.

Upon graduating with a B.S. in Finance and a Master's Degree in Coaching & Athletic Administration Anthony began assisting several student-athletes with their recruiting process. Anthony noticed that there was something missing for those athletes and their families who wanted to play sports in college. Anthony wrote a how to guide known as The Top Recruit to assist families with their recruitment. The Top Recruit is a detailed perspective that covers the recruiting cycle from a recruiters, student-athlete and parent perspective. The expertise in the book comes from interviews from several collegiate athletes, college coaches and student-athletes. Recently Anthony also coached at Episcopal High School the home of two 5 star recruits. Anthony has professional relationships with coaches from the Big Ten, Big 12, SEC, ACC, Pac 12, Ivy League and Division 2 & 3 schools. Their expert opinion and conversations are paraphrased throughout the book. Anthony has also trained, coached and mentored over 1000 student-athletes with some of his athletes receiving scholarship offers from LSU, Ole Miss, Indiana, Cal Berkeley, Harvard, Yale, Columbia, TCU, Baylor, and Nebraska to name a few. Anthony has also drew content from his peers while also recalling conversation throughout training sessions with some of the best professional athletes in the world including:

- Mike Wallace - Baltimore Ravens/Ole Miss
- Jerrod Johnson -NFL Quarterback/Texas A&M
- Weldon Brown - Jacksonville Jaguars/La.Tech/CFL
- McCollins Umeh - Arizona Wildcats

- Deon Murphy - Kansas State/CFL
- Bryan Pittman - Houston Texans
- Brian Dozier - Minnesota Twins/Southern Miss
- Patrick Jackson - Louisiana Tech
- Jordan Jefferson - LSU
- Adam Pac-Man Jones - Pro Bowl Cornerback/WVU
- Josh Barvin - Cornell
- Dustin Mitchell - New Orleans Saints/La.Tech
- Daniel Porter - CFL Star/La.Tech
- Rashad Lewis - NBA Champion
- Mike James - NBA Star/ Duquesne
- Jonathan Holland - Oakland Raiders/La.Tech
- Will Thanheiser - Princeton
- Anthony James - St. Louis Rams/La.Tech
- Fendi Onobun - St. Louis Rams/Arizona
- Kendrick Lewis - Baltimore Ravens/Ole Miss
- Dominic Patrick - Arizona/NFL/UFL
- Bradley McDougald - Seattle Seahawks/Kansas University

DEDICATION

This book is dedicated to those who dare to dream. I believe in you, you believe in yourself and most importantly God put a dream in your heart. Chase your dreams wide awake with belief and a relentless work ethic. Also, to my beautiful wife Ashley, thank you.

CONTENTS

PROLOGUE

Going through the recruiting process can be a very blissful time in a student-athlete's life. Having many of the country's top universities contact you and your family can be very exciting. In fact, being wanted by just one university can be quite flattering. However, recruiting can also become stressful to the student-athlete and their family. It is important to stay in control and well-grounded throughout this process, because ultimately you are still the one in control of your decisions. After all, a student-athlete can compete and earn a degree at only one university at a time. No two recruiting processes will be the same, so enjoy the recruitment journey and the process that comes with it.

While the athlete takes this journey, it is essential to consider the dual role in which they will play, that being the student and athlete, with the student hat yielding top priority. Moreover, the merger of these two roles assumes that a student-athlete follow rules, especially those required to maintain a good academic standing, as well as not taking part in unethical or illegal activities. The journey on which I will guide you in the following seven chapters will be informative, perhaps even insightful, and hopefully prompt questions such as

1. **"How can I promote myself to get my name out there to coaches and recruiters?"**
2. **"What is considered a full scholarship?"**
3. **"How quickly should I accept an offer not from my top school?"**
4. **"How can I solicit more scholarships?**
5. **"My friend is getting letters and scholarship offers, but I am not. What can I do to also get recruited?"**

While addressing details about recruiting, I will also share some things your local high school coaches may not tell you. Furthermore, because most families are experiencing this process for the first time, I will tackle topics from multiple perspectives: student- athlete, parental, and college coach/recruiter's, each designed to help you to more fully understand the complexities with which recruitment is associated.

This book does not guarantee you a scholarship, but it will allow you to increase your chances for securing a scholarship and in signing that covetous national letter of intent. This is indeed a process, one that requires enormous patience, tenacity, and faith. In short, these important decisions that you make can affect everything from who you will marry, what career you pursue, and even the makeup of your future generations.

Be patient throughout the journey and remember it does not matter if you have seventy offers or one; you can only attend one university at a time. You only need one!

CHAPTER ONE

GRADES MATTER

Student-Athlete

Remember "Student-athlete" is written that way for a reason: Student comes first. Get it? I do not care how talented you are, how fast you run or how many touchdowns you have scored. If you can't read, write, speak, think, and act like a college graduate, you will not play on Saturdays. And how can you? You'll be swamped with tutors trying to keep you from flunking out of school. Until you stop daydreaming in class, your true dream of playing college football or any other sport, will not happen. In order to compete athletically in college, you have to receive admission into the university. Each university has its own criteria for admission. Your first task is to get in and stay in!

Block out distractions

It is estimated that about 6% of all high school athletes will compete in NCAA after high school. For more popular American sports like football and basketball, that number is even less. Your lofty dream can come true if you erase all the psychological, physical, and environmental distractions that get in the way. Sure, make friends, have fun, make memories. But make sure the memories you create are those that will help to shape your future. Everything you do in school, every decision you make is like making a deposit. Each deposit should yield interest. If you are not getting interest from your deposits (i.e., those good decisions you make about time well-spent), then your investment will crack. You do want to invest in your career, right? You do look for that payoff, right? You are planning to be one of the small percentage of student-athletes that "make it," right? To increase the probability that you are in that small percentage you need to establish a set of clear priorities with one word leading the list: Study. Your athleticism and determination are all important, but unless you make studying your top priority, your athletic career will probably not come to fruition. Don't get me wrong, because studying alone doesn't create a sense of balance in your life. But a strict regimen of study habits fueled by sound time management on your part should rule your life.

If completing homework assignments and studying for tests are challenging for you, then adjust your circle of friends and hang with students who strive for excellence in the classroom. Find ways to make homework assignments fun and interactive and get the proper tutoring if needed. This might sound boring but, if done correctly , it will pay big dividends in the long run.

What Recruiters Ask

One of the first questions I get when talking to college coaches has little to do with a person's athletic ability. Rather it has to do with the recruit's G.P.A. and scores on the ACT and SAT. These conversations happen for a good reason: They are predictors. And coaches like to make predictions. They see you as a person on whom they are placing a bet; and an expensive bet at that. If you are too much of a risk, say your grades and your scores, then your overall academic ability is suspect. You want to slam the door on any doubts. Grades. Talent. You got it all. Get into that university and engage that coach with the "Wow" factor, that being the total student-athlete. Show that coach you play both those roles well. When playing both roles know this: You are preparing for life, not only a career. Athletes such as Myron Rolle,

Shane Battier, Steve Young, Dawn Staley, Cheryl Miller, Kristin Day,Ryan Fitzpatrick, Pau Gasol and Emeka Okafor are just a few of highly successful professional athletes, who also excelled in academics. If you never heard of these athletes then I suggest you look them up. You'll be impressed. And in case you're not following my train of thought, I am telling you that it's a good idea to aspire to be on this list too. And you are off to good start because you have incentive. Incentive is a first step in making things happen, including those strategies for doing the best that you can in the classroom. As that motivated, hard-driven athlete, be sure to take advantage of the resources that your local school and community provide. Tutorials, ACT and SAT prep, and after-school programs should be utilized. Know the location and contact person of the resources you require. "Who is your guidance counselor?" "Who are the students that can help you with your homework?" "Which teachers will assist you, going out of their way to encourage and motivate you?" Don't hesitate to look outside of your school. In Houston, Texas, our local community college offers free tutoring for SAT prep. Do your research and find the programs you need. Trying to do the least amount of work for the best possible grade is not the way to go through your high school years. Is that what you'd do on the field? Give it your "least?" I didn't think so. By aiming to be the best version of yourself and having the best grades possible, you can make a recruiter's job easier. YOU will be the one they want.

My SAT Story

For myself, going to a private school definitely helped. At my private school our course curriculum included an allotted time to go over SAT material. This assisted in my development and desire to score the best score possible. Our guidance counselor also demanded that we take the ACT/SAT our junior year of high school. I ended up taking the SAT in the spring of my junior year and once in the summer that year, all before my senior year of high school. This helped out tremendously in the recruiting process. I recall going to visit TCU (Texas Christian University) on an unofficial visit and the coaching staff bragged on me in front of all the other top recruits because of my high SAT score. I felt proud, because not only was my athletic performance on point, but I had the grades and SAT score to validate my ability to succeed in college. None of this came easily. I had to learn to do it, and that is my simple and hopefully profound advice to you: You must learn it. Here are some key ideas to point you in the right direction.

What Should I be Doing about the ACT or SAT

As early as your freshman year in high school, sit down with a guidance counselor, trusted teacher, or family member and begin taking the practice ACT or practice SAT. The practice test is a way for you to become familiar with questions that will appear on the test and aide you in making the highest score possible once you take the official test. As an athlete, would you run a forty yard dash in front of scouts without practicing first? Of course not. The ACT and SAT are only offered at certain times of the year, so make sure you go online and register for the test. Preferably, the test should be taken during the off-season before your senior year of high school. Taking the test during the off-season will allow the student-athlete to be more alert and attentive to the test while taking it. And take it early because if you don't like your score, you can take it again. Let me add that one of the urgent set of academic skills you want to develop are spoken and written communication skills. After all, no matter what you know, or even how brilliant you may be, if you cannot say it and write it clearly, you might as well keep thoughts to yourself because no one will know what you're talking about. Therefore, learn to write and speak clearly and effectively. You will certainly need to take English courses in college, and probably a public speaking course as well. Those classes are good ways to acquire these important skills, but think about practicing your communication skills as often as you can outside the classroom.

Don't let Anything Get in the Way

I understand that everyone will not have the good fortunate that I had when applying to college. Research the internet on times and locations for the standardized tests. Some students even have their registration fee waived, especially if enrolled in the Federal National School Lunch Program (NSLP), if the family receives public assistance, if a resident of public housing or foster care, or a variety of other possibilities. Do not allow money or time to be an excuse for you not to invest in your future. If you can buy a new pair of kicks then you can find a way to pay for a much needed tutorial session or standardized test.

NCAA Eligibility Center

The NCAA Eligibility Center (formerly known as the NCAA Clearinghouse) is the branch that oversees athletic eligibility throughout your college athletic career. It is important that you register with the Eligibility Center your junior year of high school and find out what high school course requirements you may need. If you know at an early age that you want to compete at the university level, then you would want to meet with your academic advisor to make sure you are taking the courses required by the Eligibility Center your freshman or sophomore year of high school. There is a fee to register for the Eligibility Center which is currently $70 for U.S. and Canadian athletes and $120 for international athletes. You can get a fee waiver through your academic advisor at your high school if needed. Have your standardized test scores mailed to the Eligibility Center or have the testing center send it directly to the Eligibility Center. You will also need official transcripts sent to the Eligibility Center. If you have attended multiple high schools, all official transcripts will need to be sent. Know that registering with the Eligibility Center does not get you recruited. It makes sure that you are academically eligible to compete at a NCAA DI or DII program.

To be clear, here are the steps to follow:

1. Meet with academic advisor or academic counselor.
2. Register with the Eligibility Center.
3. Send official transcripts to the Eligibility Center.
4. Send ACT/SAT scores to the Eligibility Center.
5. Take the correct classes to be academically eligible at the next level.
6. Follow up with academic advisor or academic counselor.

Parents

Parents, it is so important that you emphasize the importance to your student- athlete to be well-rounded as well as accountable. You know, every student-athlete need to have a sense of ownership, an ability to take responsibility. And this accountability is a byproduct of being well-rounded. Being a recruited athlete can come with perks that can be beneficial to your athlete, but they can also be harmful. Make sure your student-athlete is responsible and held accountable for their work. You know that these skills are essential to becoming an a productive adult. If they cut corners now then there is a high probability that they will cut corners as an adult. Emphasize the importance of education. Some of you may think that education is not the key to a successful life, but it does unlock more doors than you ever dreamed possible. Even if your son is a Top Recruit and is rated a 5-star prospect by all the recruiting agencies, you must continue to emphasize how a good education will help in becoming a well-rounded person.

Every student will not make straight A's, but every student should do the very best they can, and that is precisely what we need to make clear to student-athletes. Parents need to convey to their student-athletes that "winning," isn't about being the best at all costs; rather it's about being the best you can be all of the time. Punctuate the importance of working toward a good G.P.A. in high school and, of course, continue that advice when the athlete goes to college. As a parent, it is also important that you get involved in school by asking about assignments, exploring a variety of interests, and inquiring if any help is needed with homework. Getting involved is the only viable way to express both encouragement and support, not to mention a very cool loving gesture for the student-athlete in your life.

Parents can't be expected to know everything about the recruitment process, and that includes the academic prerequisites that come with it. It's important to recognize that it is okay, and in fact normal not to know about the ACT or SAT process. Contact the athlete's guidance counselor or academic advisor. Follow this up with a teacher or administrator so you can become better informed of the process. During this time period, identify an ACT/SAT tutor to inform about everything from testing locations to preparatory resources. Be proactive during every step of the way. Make sure that the student-athlete is registered with the NCAA Eligibility Center by his or her junior year. Meet with an academic advisor to make sure the student-athlete is taking the required coursework to be eligible for and NCAA DI or DII programs.

Recruiter's Point of View

Recruiters want to recruit the best talent possible. Certain universities including the Ivy League schools, Division III universities, and private universities utilize the academic qualifying process over athletic ability to determine if they can offer a perspective student-athlete. Academics are priority at these universities. If a perspective student athlete cannot meet the minimum requirements to enroll at the university their talent cannot gain them admission. I have seen with my own eyes a coach offer a perspective student athlete early in the process (junior year of high school) and then withdraw the offer from the perspective student-athlete' there senior year because of academics. Coaches and recruiters do not want to do this, but it is part of the business side of athletics. Make it easy on recruiters and do your part.

CHAPTER TWO

CALENDAR

Dear Student-Athlete. I'm Talking to YOU

It is time to start thinking about becoming a student-athlete the moment you begin you freshman year in high school. Although your size, speed, weight, and overall athleticism might not be on par with college level competition, you must plan to work hard to get that level. I cannot overstate the importance of starting strong by receiving the best grades you can at the end of your first semester. Work hard to get A's, but more important, earn them fairly. Being the best student you can be will create chances for scholarships and, as a result, inflate your options. You don't want recruiters waiting for your G.P.A. to improve, and you certainly don't want them to view you as a poor student. That news can spread faster than a forest fire.

Prove to them you mean business NOW! Clearly, if your freshman year turns out to be weaker than expected, you can build momentum during your sophomore, and maybe junior year. But the longer you wait, the harder it becomes. If you wait too long to get your academics up to speed, you will find your dreams of becoming a professional athlete disappear. A's and B's. Sure, it's never too late to improve. But in your case, the window closes a bit faster than for others. My advice is simple: Don't worry about finding ways to improve. Work Hard Now!

When Can a Recruiter Reach-Out

Recruiters are not allowed to contact you anytime they want. There are restrictions placed on coaches and recruiters imposed by the NCAA. There are designated time periods throughout your high school career when a recruiter can contact you. If the recruiter does not respond to an email, text message, or direct message then there could be a reason behind it. For guidance, I have listed and defined a variety of items which are limited by the NCAA during various times of the year, including periods of contact, periods of evaluation, quiet periods labeled as periods of "quiet," periods seen as "dead," and a calendar that documents periods of recruitment. Let me give you a feel for each period:

Grades 9 & 10:

A recruit can receive only the following material: Camp Brochures, questionnaires, NCAA publications, and non-athletic institutional publications.

Grade 11:

A recruit can receive recruiting materials, including electronical material (e.g., email). All forms of private communication for football are permitted beginning September 1st. One personal telephone call about football is permitted between April 15th and May 31st. It is imperative that all recruits go online and research which rules apply to which sport, including the sport-specific calendar with which those rules come.

Grade 12:

One telephone call per week are allowed for football after September 1st. During the period, a coach and/or recruiter can have unlimited contact with the student-athlete. At an unlimited rate.

Official Visit:

A recruit will receive a maximum of 5 official visits. Any visit to a college campus that is paid for by the college is considered an official visit.

Contact period:

Coaches are allowed to visit with student-athletes and their families. During the pre-season, contact is limited to one time per week. Coaches are not allowed to visit a school multiple times in one week. Email, electronic communications, and written communication are also permitted during this time. Coaches tend to set up in home visits to visit recruits and their families as it gets closer to signing day.

Evaluation period:

Face to face contact is not allowed. Home visits are off limits. Coaches are allowed to visit the student-athlete's school in order to evaluate the prospect. Throughout the evaluation period, many scholarships are offered, and both electronic and written communication are allowed.

Quiet period:

Off campus contact is not allowed. During the quiet period the student-athlete can visit the university's campus and receive written and electronic communication. If it is the spring or summer, coaches will invite the student-athlete to unofficially visit the university.

Dead period:

This is the most restrictive time during the recruiting phase. No face to face contact is allowed for an on campus visit or off campus visit for a prospective student-athlete. Written and electronic email is accepted.

About the Recruiting Calendar:

The NCAA recruiting calendar can be a little confusing. Go online and look at your perspective sport to understand what is appropriate and what is not. Using 2015-2016 as an example, on the next page is a simplified version for football though it changes slightly from year to year. Know at all times what period you are in and what can take place during this time. Keeping a visible calendar in sight will be helpful in determining when you can receive contact from coaches.

Date and period	Visit prospect's school	Visit prospect outside of school	Prospect can visit university & meet w/ coaches
8/1/15 - 11/28/15 Quiet Period			✓
9/1/15 - 11/30/15 Evaluation (42 select days)	✓		✓
11/29/15 - 12/13/15 Contact Period	✓	✓	✓
12/14/15 - 1/13/16 Dead Period			
1/14/16 - 1/30/16 Contact Period	✓	✓	✓
1/31/16 Quiet Period			✓
2/1/16 - 2/4/16 Dead Period			
2/5/16 - 4/14/16 Quiet Period			✓
4/15/16- 5/31/16 Evaluation Period	✓		✓
6/1/16 - 6/26/16 Quiet Period			✓
6/27/16 - 7/10/16 Dead Period			
7/11/16 - 7/31/16 Quiet Period			✓

Parents

Pay close attention to the dates mentioned in the student-athlete section of this chapter. As a parent, you want to hold the student-athlete responsible for knowing when to appropriately contact a coach. You also want to know what camps the student-athlete should be attending, when they should be taking their placement test, and the importance of being proactive throughout the process. One thing you want to keep in mind is that there are a limited number of scholarships that a university will give out in comparison to the number of high school athletes trying to earn a scholarship. Consider the job search as an analogy:. If you recently graduated from college and began looking for a job, you would not wait until the last minute. You would begin immediately, including visits to job fairs, sending out resumes, composing great cover letters, etc. If you retained a headhunter, would you place full responsibility on him for getting you a job? Of course not. That said, don't wait until the last minute to start promoting the student-athlete. Make sure the summer camps attended by the student-athlete is sponsored by a university. Complete online questionnaires, and send promotional material about your student-athlete. Know all the deadlines and time periods to contact coaches and apply for scholarships (Division II and Division III). Be aware of head hunters who act as a liaison between the student-athlete and the coach. Coaches may try to contact your student-athlete at 7.a.m. or contact them late in the evening all throughout the week. If the student-athlete has homework and other things to prepare for, feel free to talk to the coach, or ask him to call back another day. Set boundaries, and then adhere to them and enjoy the process.

Recruiter's Point of View

Because of their innate competitive nature, recruiters try to attract the best talent to fill the athletic needs in the programs of various universities. While most recruiters are aware of restrictions imposed by the NCAA, they are also able to find the loop holes needed to contact a prospective student-athlete. They will often encourage you all to come visit the campus, to call them any time, and extend a seemingly generous open invitation to come to an athletic competition any time you wish. Don't be duped by this. College coaches are mostly terrific people and, more important, very ethical people who respect the guidelines set by the NCAA. It is important for student-athletes to also respect NCAA guidelines so they can stay eligible. Recognize that recruiters typically do not ignore you. Like you, they cannot answer every call, respond to every text or email. They're like any busy person responsible for family, illnesses, travel, and the like. The proverbial bottom line is this: Maintain the integrity of the recruitment process because it absolutely the right thing to do.

CHAPTER THREE

PROMOTION

One of the biggest myths is, "My coach is sending out my film." Although this might be true, it is not your high school's coach's job to send your film to universities. Their primary function is to win games for the sport they represent. Because their job depends largely on winning, that coach will focus time and attention on winning at all costs, making sure they keep their jobs.

Your high school coach has an abundance of responsibilities and an overwhelming number of student-athletes. The coach orchestrates budgets, fields busy calendars, and manages a coaching staff, just to name a few. That coach might simply forget to send out your film. Simply put, if you do not get recruited or promoted, do not place the blame on coaches. It is your job to promote yourself. It is your job to send film to coaching staffs and recruiters. It is your job to make good grades and take the required courses needed to attend a specific university. It is your job to construct a highlight tape that solicits the attention of these recruiters. It is your job to demonstrate good character, and to show respect to your coaches, teachers and administrators.

Student-Athlete

The word, interview, means "viewing internally." Therefore, it is not a stretch to imagine every game as an interview. Putting together good plays on video is an effective way of making sure that you grab the attention of college recruiters, not unlike that terrific attention-getter you might use in an interview. Recruiters often look at what you are doing when you are not getting the ball and not the center of attention. Are you demonstrating leadership and professionalism? Are you indeed a team player? What do your gestures and actions convey? Additionally, configure a 2-4 minute highlight tape that spotlights your best plays from the season. Think of these plays as "Wow plays." These plays are the type not seen every day—the kind of plays that showcase your potential for university-level athletics. And you need "Wow" plays in high school because if you have no remarkable plays to illustrate , there will be little chance a coach will imagine you will make them stellar plays in college. Make those plays: See them in your mind, feel them in your bones, and develop the determination to make them happen.

If for whatever reason you cannot produce an impressive highlight tape, then consider a workout tape. This tape should show the recruiter what special skills and traits you possess. For example, if you are 5'5 and 140 pounds, you still can be recruited by , say, a football coach, but you better make it crystal clear that your speed, strength, and maneuverability are electrifying. , You guessed it: You want the coach to say, "Wow!" If you want to play volleyball and stand 6'1, then creatively show the recruiter how your height can be an advantage. I have seen student-athletes recruited by doing some of the most spectacular things, like jumping out of a pool, throwing a football up in the air and running 40 yards to catch it; or even jumping over bags that were 60 inches tall. Use your visible strengths and explore avenues to display those strengths. Be sure you have access to a smart phone, an iPad, or go to your l school's library and checkout a camcorder. If you want a recruiter and the university to invest thousands of dollars in you, then do your part by investing in yourself.

Social Media

Use technology to your advantage. Promote yourself on Twitter, Facebook, and Instagram. Do your part by using Hudl and the many other online sources. From now until you start your first day of college, your social media page should be used to expose your athletic talents, including those developed in extra-curricular activities.

Because social media is all about exposed expression, watch your language. No swearing or off-color words. Be thoughtful when you speak. Sound interesting and colorful by expressing yourself clearly and enthusiastically. Don't tweet stupid thoughts and derogatory statements. If you are thinking about posting illegal activities, then think again. Don't embarrass yourself, insult anyone, or showcase the kind of character and judgment with which a coach (and players) will never want to be associated. After all, would you want your mother to see you in "bad form?" I didn't think so. Then why would we want to show it to coaches, recruiters, and other players. When you prove yourself thoughtful and intelligent on social media, you demonstrate the very best you can be. And that is NEVER wrong.

Positive Promotion can go a Long Way

Here are some social media posts that are clear, upbeat, and intelligent. Words are chosen wisely, and truthful messages are told. Here are some illustrations:

- **A Letter from the University of Michigan. #GoBigBlue**
- **I want to thank the University of Arkansas Pine Buff for my 1st offer. I am thankful and grateful. #Blessed #D1Bound #NCAA #FirstOffer**
- **@Coach Harris from Tulane in New Orleans It is a pleasure to see the success of your program, and I look forward to getting to know you and more about the University soon.**
- **WOW! What a night! 10 catches, 150 yards, 1 touchdown, and 5 tackles. Thank you to my team and coaches for a big time win vs. the number 10 team in the state.**

Do you notice the common denominators in these posts? It's all promotion, sure. More important, it's all positive. Things to consider: Only use pictures that represent your school, university, and achievements in a positive way. Some universities have an entire department dedicated exclusively to watch for posts on social media that inform them about both current and prospective student-athletes. I have seen student-athletes lose a scholarship offer because of one dumb tweet or bad Instagram. Do NOT be that person. You are no longer a typical teenager. You represent something bigger and hopefully better. You must showcase yourself as a responsible, reliable, and determined individual. If you want to impress girls or make political statements, then find a delivery system no one, and I mean no one can access through social media. And don't even think about posting anything that comes within waving distance of violence, hostility, or the like. Nothing will destroy your dreams faster and more permanently than being viewed as a dangerous or intimidating young man.

Parental Note

Please support your child if he wants to take part in extracurricular activities in college. Learning an instrument, becoming a dancer, debating on the college debate team, even playing chess, writing poems, and acting in a play can all yield partial scholarships, not to mention help shape your student-athlete into a well-rounded, culturally-oriented person. These stories validate this point of view:

Jennifer's Story

Jennifer is one of my former athletes. In high school, Jennifer was a standout athlete, involved in many extracurricular activities. Jennifer competed as a volleyball player and softball player while also being a part of the drama club, the debate team, and the FFA (Future Farmers of America). Jennifer's achievements were enough to earn her recognition by many universities. But due to budget constraints and limited scholarships, Jennifer did not receive a full scholarship to any university. However, Jennifer's story was awesome, nevertheless. With a grade point average of 3.75, she received a $5,000 scholarship. She also received another $10,000 from the FFA, and the university's athletic department (softball team) decided to pay for her room and board, out of state fees, and cover all costs for her books.

There really are many ways to receive financial assistance for your student-athlete, but it requires research and perseverance. You haven't done this before and you must start somewhere. Why not Google "scholarships?" You will be astonished at the number of items that surface. The counselors at your child's school are more resourceful than you think, and don't forget to ask parents who've been through this before. They have lots of advice and wisdom they would be happy to share. In short, don't make it a secret that you are researching scholarship possibilities.

Seeing is Believing

You've heard the adage, "Dress to impress?" Well, change it to "Film to impress." Film relevant events, honors, speeches, award ceremonies, and of course athletic feats of greatness. Smart phones, IPads, camcorders, even written journal entries can help to document those moments of grandeur. You might consider hiring a professional videographer, another student with videography "know-how," or even you're your other kids with that cinematic ambition. A film is like a sample of what is purchased; a powerful visual representation of a "product" in need.

If you've ever been job hunting, you know about the power behind a resume. And your resume is powerful because you spent time crafting it that way. Filming your student-athlete is precisely the same thing. It is their resume, and because it is visual, it shows an animated athlete and a hard copy of measurable achievements.

That is something no other medium can offer. It is that powerful. to send out a hard copy of their achievements.

To accompany this visual hard-copy is the standard resume done right. Resumes should focus on the student-athlete's activities, awards, and accomplishments. This resume should also include their height, weight, positive comments made about the student athlete in articles written about him, and references composed by credible coaches. Be creative. This is your first impression and a chance to sell the student-athlete while soliciting interest from a university and its staff. Go online and find the questionnaires for the universities in which you are interested. Complete the questionnaire and demonstrate to the university that you are interested in their program. Please look at Appendix A for an example of a cover letter and Appendix B for a sample resume.

Parents and Student-Athletes

My Promotion Story

I can remember it like it was yesterday. The day after my high school football games, I would come in and ask my coach to borrow the tape over the weekend. He would often say yes, and then I would take that video home and connect two televisions to each other. In doing so, I would take a blank tape and record the game on one of those tapes. Then I would take another tape and record my highlight plays! I did that for 10 weeks straight. It was time consuming and tough, but I had a goal in mind. I did not take no for an answer. If coach did not let me get the tapes after the games, I would simply wait until the middle of the week when I knew he would say yes. After a while he knew my routine and would have a copy waiting for me on Saturdays!

I've heard this statement used too many times: "My coach was supposed to send my film out but he did not." And I've witnessed it firsthand too. It is important that you all take responsibility for the student-athletes future. Using social media can be extremely helpful. If the student-athlete is not responsible enough, the parent can create an account for them and use this to promote athletic achievements. Also go online and fill out a recruiting questionnaire to as many universities as possible. Most universities will have a questionnaire on their online sports portal for perspective student-athletes to fill out.

Jackson's Story

Jackson, who was one of the top 3 quarterbacks in the state of Texas received letters and phone calls from across the nation, universities including: Northwestern, Brown, Stanford, Central Florida, Michigan, Memphis, and Oklahoma State were all highly interested in this outstanding student-athlete. But before Jackson's senior year of high school he was not offered a scholarship. Unlike other recruits, Jackson did his part, contacting coaches weekly by email and phone calls. Jackson also kept a list of recruiters who had visited his school during his sophomore and junior year of high school and what coaches continued building a relationship with him throughout his high school tenure. Jackson often sent letters, film and inquiries to universities but going into his senior year Jackson did not have one scholarship offer. To make things worse, Jackson's offensive coordinator Coach Smith did not assist him in the recruiting process. Jackson would later find out that when recruiters from these top tier universities would call and visit Coach Smith, he would speak very little about Jackson but instead he would shift the conversation and focus on Luke, a wide receiver and family friend who was a good player who doubled as Jackson's good friend and teammate. When Jackson heard of this information he was devastated. But Jackson remained patient throughout the process and received a full athletic scholarship to one of the best Division I universities. Jackson went on to earn several accolades as a collegiate athlete also. In this case Jackson did not let his coach or emotions get the best of him. Instead Jackson stayed the course and kept promoting and being a good student in order to achieve his goal of being a scholarship student-athlete.

Recruiter's Point of View

During the recruiting phase, it is normal for a university to send out letters, camp invitations, and emails to student-athletes. Letters are usually an introduction to the student-athlete, and it implies that there is interest in the athlete by the university and its coaching staff. This letter or email is usually a letter of interest identifying the recruit is a potential target, and that the staff will be diligently scouting and interacting with the student-athlete. In the months to come, the recruiter may look at the recruit's credentials, focusing on grades, signs of character, statistics, and his social media profile. This is not a scholarship, but rather one step in the recruitment process and an informal way of meeting and hopefully initiating a long-term relationship between the recruiter, the recruit, and the family involved in making the final decision.

Recruiters also use camps as a way to promote their university and to identify top recruits. These camps usually take place in two ways. The first is on campus during the summer months. The purpose is to get interested prospects an unofficial look of the campus, its athletic program, and the town in which it is located. The other camp is a one-day mini-camp. This camp, known as a satellite camp, usually takes place in the main recruiting area in which the university recruits. This camp serves as an opportunity for recruiters to get an up-close and personal look at several student-athletes. This is a chance recruiters use to build relationships, identify new talent, and cultivate relationships with student athletes with whom they already know.

Finally, recruiters send emails, media guides, and letters to the recruit's home, school, and various online message forums. Again, this is a chance for the recruiter and university to continue their ongoing relationship.

CHAPTER FOUR

CAMPS & SKILL-TRAINING

Student-Athlete

I get it; Social media outlets like Instagram, Twitter, Periscope, and Facebook, creates a desire for instant gratification. As a student-athlete, it is very stressful to see your childhood friends get recruiting letters and scholarship offers while you continue to wait for the same attention. By looking at their social media, it is easy to think that their last Twitter post earned them a scholarship. While it may appear that way, it is not true. Most of the top athletes earn a scholarship based on their potential and in having that special quality not found in other student-athletes. For example, if a student-athlete stands 6'3 and weighs 275 pounds while wearing a size 14 shoe and is 14 years old in the 9th grade, most recruiters will project the student-athlete to reach 6'6 in height and weight 315 pounds. This is an ideal size for an offensive lineman at the college level. At this moment he may not be strong, he may not be fast, but according to historical data used to make sound predictions, he has the potential to develop into a solid athlete if cultivated at the right university program. Although you may currently be more athletically talented, the previously mentioned student-athlete has something you cannot teach: Size. Size and speed cannot be taught, and both are traits coaches look for when recruiting. I encourage all student-athletes to continue to strive to become better at those things that can be controlled. Just because you are not an ideal size for one university does not mean that there is not a program out there for you. Continue to work hard and develop your skills and learn the necessary tools to help you get recruited.

What Should I be Doing?

One of the key questions I receive almost daily about being recruited is "What should I be doing?" The answer? You should be working. Playing video games and sitting on the couch praying for a scholarship is not the answer. If your goal is to play a sport in college, you must be putting in the proper amount of work. Although you may be the best athlete at your school, you are competing against more than just the people at your school. You are competing against the thousands of other student-athletes in your state and from across the country who have the same dream of earning a scholarship. Part of working is making sure that you are trained by the right people.

Athletic Performance Facility

If you live in cities like Houston, Dallas, Miami, Orlando, Los Angeles or Phoenix, finding an athletic facility is easy. If an athletic facility is near you, I suggest you train there. Most athletic facilities have trainers who are quite knowledgeable and know how to push student-athletes to the next level. Many of these trainers are ex-athletes or certified athletic trainers who are very knowledgeable and are dedicated to their craft. Their goal is to get you better and they are rewarded by seeing you sign that athletic scholarship of your choice.

If you are deciding between two facilities, don't be afraid to train at both. One may offer a better speed workout, while the other offers better explosion drills. There is nothing wrong with seeking out multiple forms of training to gain an athletic advantage. Figure out what works best for you and put in the proper work to be successful. Athletic facilities are great places to train because of the competition level. Being around the best athletes in the game is inspiring and it helps to see what others are doing to be great. Being at this facility will also help your drive to become better. Many times, you will be paired with a group of guys who are on the same mission as you. Therefore, you guys will challenge each other daily during your training regimen.

Training Story (NFL , NBA & MLB Legends)

I remember it like it was yesterday. During my sophomore year in high school, I heard from someone that there was an athletic facility opening on the south-side of Houston, Texas. *Being from the north-side and going to school near mid-town, the commute to this athletic facility was over an hour. But nevertheless I asked my mother and father to go visit. My father and I drove to the other side of town, and to my amazement it was everything I could imagine and more. Driving up to the facility I saw luxury cars fixed up with big rims and sound speakers blasting. When my father and I walked into the facility, I saw many of the top athletes working out, laughing, and enjoying the grind. I immediately knew that I had to train here. After taking a quick tour, the owner told us the price and the workout plan he had in mind for me. My father asked me if this was what I wanted to do and that I would have to make the sacrifice to drive out here four times a week. I immediately said yes! On the car ride home I was so happy. For me it was like meeting the President of the United States or going on a trip to Disney World. Here I was, 15 years old and training with three of the best trainers in the world, Dr. Min Lu, Danny Arnold, and Champ Glory.*

These guys had trained 1st round draft picks, Super Bowl champions, and Heisman trophy winners. I ended up training with Heisman Trophy Winner and Super Bowl Champion Charles Woodson, who is now an ESPN analyst. I trained with Casey Hampton, a University of Texas legend and Super Bowl Champion and even Rashad Lewis, a Houston Texas High School Legend, NBA Champion and all-star basketball player. Over the years I worked alongside or trained with Tracy McGrady (NBA Superstar), Jake Matthews (NFL – ALL Pro) member of the famous Matthews Family, Julius Peppers (All-Pro NFL Player), and countless of other superstars. The environment was amazing, competition was always high, music was upbeat, and the athletes were all striving to get better. Not only did I get a chance to train with some of the best athletes in the world, I trained with my peers; I trained with 3, 4 and 5 star recruits all on the same mission: to dominate high school and earn a full scholarship to the university of their choice. Till this day the sacrifice my parents made for me to train at Plex was one of the best decisions of my life. I can honestly say that I would not have been as successful on the field if I had not trained with some of the best athletes in the world.

Skills Training

If you live in a small town that does not have the luxury of an athletic performance facility, or live in a city where the commute is too long, then finding a skills coach is your best option. With the rise of social media and free advertising, it is easier than you think to locate skill coaches in most towns, who can help you develop your talent. Like the athletic facility trainer, these coaches are usually former players who are looking to make a difference in their local athletic community. If you are a basketball player looking to improve your jump shot, find a coach that can help you with that. If you are a baseball player and you want to work on some speed training then find a track coach or speed coach that can assist you develop those set of skills.

The great thing about skill coaches is that they may be more affordable, because they do not have the overhead of a facility. They can also be more personable, offering a more customized one-on-one training, or even smaller group sessions. You will want to find a coach with the personality that best fits your needs. Not everyone is for everybody.

If you do not like the training given by your coach, then find a coach with whom you can work. Look, you can decide on the style best suited for you. You are the one who needs to learn and develop so you better like the coach who is charged with leading you down that path. If you decide to leave a coach, find an appropriate way to communicate that or have your parents tell them why you have decided to go in a different direction. Keep in mind there can have two good people who do not necessarily belong together. That's perfectly alright. If you think a coach isn't fully invested in developing your talent but is instead only interested in taking your money, then find someone else. Most skill coaches truly care about your development and want to see you grow as an athlete. Find the right one to help take your game to the next level.

Camps

The most common question I receive about camps is "What camps should I be attending?" This can be a tricky question because the answer depends on your personal goals. There are several different camps out there for high school athletes that can be beneficial, including showcase camps, exposure camps, college one-day camps, team camps, sport-specific camps (like 7v7 camps), and lineman camps. These each have a different purpose, so I will briefly provide a description of each type. Keep in mind that many of these camps cost money. When coupled with the costs in athletic training, traveling, gas, hotel accommodations, and meals, camp life can add up to some serious green. The mature and sensible student-athlete will sit down with his parents, guardians, and coaches, and determine which camps will be helpful and affordable.

Showcase Camps and Exposure Camps

These camps can be very helpful because they embrace a great deal of media coverage on the premises. The writers from Rivals, 247, scout.com, ESPN, and other media outlets are typically at these events. Clearly, showing yourself well in this environment can help you gain terrific exposure to a number of college coaches. Do not worry if you have a bad camp, because there are other factors included when a college decides to offer you a scholarship. I recommend going to these camps early during your high school career (9th & 10th grade), or even in middle school so you can better gauge the competition. I also recommend these camps if you have been training and have the ability to perform well in front of evaluators. Don't even think about attending these camps if you are injured or out of shape.

For your information: The typical showcase camp/exposure camps can start as low as $20 to as much as $325.

One-Day College Camps

One-day camps are being called many different things nowadays. Oftentimes these one-day camps are camps sponsored by the university. These camps are great for high school juniors and seniors and provide an opportunity for recruits to be coached and noticed by college coaches. These camps are a good way for the coach and student-athlete relationship to be developed. These camps sometimes feature several universities, with one major university being the host while several other universities will participate in scouting the top players in that region. These one-day camps, also known as satellite camps, can be regional, while others take place at their perspective university. These camps range from $25 to $80 typically. There are no excuses for a student-athlete to not attend one of these camps. If you live in a major city and play a prominent sport, these camps often come to a local high school in your area. Try to go to as many of these camps as possible and build a relationship with your position coach or coach that recruits your area.

Team Camps

Team camps are held at local universities. These camps are usually recommended by your head coach and require that you and your current teammates participate. Someone will constantly be watching you when working out at a university. Therefore, be ready to compete at the highest level you can because coaches will be watching you carefully. Also be on the alert for opposing high school coaches watching just as intently, all of whom have connections with coaches at every college in the nation. Performing well cannot be overstated. It's your performance that can win you that recommendation. Like most camps, these differ in price based on the sport and the number of participants. I recommend attending these camps as early as possible. Not only do you compete at a university campus, but you create memories that will last a lifetime and build lifelong relationships to go with them.

Sport- Specific Camps

Sport-specific camps like 7 on 7 events for football players have become more prominent in recent years. These camps are sponsored by your local state or by an athletic apparel company. These camps are often cost effective, ranging from free if by invitation, to $350 for a team, which comes to about $25 per person. These camps provide good exposure, because several recruiting websites are typically present. Be aware that these recruiting website writers typically look like the "average Joe," so always perform well because you never know who might be watching or even filming you. Exposure happens faster than a blinking eye, allowing you to go from an unknown to a well-known in virtually moments.

Parents

The camp circuit can be expensive and time consuming. But as adults, you know the importance of investing time and money to achieve that desired goal. The journey taken by your student-athletes is challenging and dynamic, and you are required to take that excursion along with them. Take the time to talk about, listen to, and learn more about the goals and dreams of your student-athlete. Make your moments together memorable and everlasting. Time stands still for no one, so before they go to college, graduate school, start a family of their own, or make you grandparents sooner than you'd like, get to know them. Understand them. Dig deep and know who they are. These are ways to enjoy the journey together.

It might be wise to create a budget that will benefit the student-athlete from year to year. Buying shoes, purchasing equipment and accessories can add up. Fast! Along with camp fees, lodging, and meals, there can be some overwhelming expenses that need to be covered. Sit down with the student-athlete and examine their goals and get a sense of their vision. This will help you budget and make appropriate decisions for the best possible solutions.

Teaming up with other parents to help get your student-athlete to camp can be a good idea, but at the end of the day do not expect others to be as invested in your student as you.

Investing in your student-athlete in the next four years, can yield wonderful memories for everyone involved.

In sum, paying $10,000 for camps, travel, and athletic expenses will be worth the investment, especially if they receive a scholarship. If school costs $40,000 a year times four years to get a degree that would equal $120,000. The $10,000 would be well worth the investment. Hiring a skills coach or training at an athletic performance facility can also cost quite a bit. Try to maximize the athlete's performance to the best of your ability. Do your homework and find what facilities, coaches, and camps will work with your budget and maximize the kid's success. Many places and trainers will work with your budget, but even if they do not, the investment in your child's success is well worth it. Ask the parents of student-athletes that have been down this road before. Know that no two student-athletes' journeys will be alike, but you can gain insight on what worked and what was not that efficient during the recruiting process. With the rise of social media, you are one direct message away from asking a question that can help you make an educated decision to help in your student-athlete's recruiting process. Finally, do not fall prey to "get rich quick" schemes done at the expense of your student-athlete. Get rich quick schemes include false promises to get your son or daughter a scholarship, don't believe it. Sometimes when we want things so badly for our children, we don't see things with open eyes. Don't shut them to these fraudulent gestures.

Story About Awareness

About three years ago, I began training a young man named Drew, a sophomore in high school and one of the better athletes in Texas. After our workout, his parents and I sat down to discuss his future goals and what was realistic for Drew. I told him that he had Division I talent and that his work ethic and future depended on what he was willing to work for. I made no promises to Drew, but encouraged him to work hard during the off-season and play his best during the football season. Drew played extremely well during his junior and senior seasons. His family began promoting Drew on social media, sent resumes to colleges, and traveled to camps during the summer. In doing so, Drew and his family were contacted by a recruiting service to have Drew evaluated for an $125.00. After the initial fee, the recruiting service told Drew he was a Division I talent. The recruiting service went on to try and sell Drew and his family one of three packages: 1.The bronze package which cost $1,000 dollars; 2.The silver package priced at $7,500; and 3. The gold package for a whopping $15,000. After feeling pressured by the *recruiting service, Drew and his family decided not to buy a package. Still, Drew eventually received serious interest from 15 Division I universities, and scholarship offers from six universities. Although, the services might have had its benefits, there are no benefits associated with high pressure "in your face" operations that are clearly motivated by cash, and not the well-being of the student-athlete. Because of their patience and keen observations, Drew and his family were able to go through the process without forking over thousands of dollars to people who may not have had Drew's best interest in mind.*

Recruiter's Point of View

Recruiters and coaches are always looking to gain a competitive edge and so should the student-athlete. Recruiters are constantly tuned into social media, watching what is being posted and if any of those posts contain stories and images of students, and with whom those students are training.. If you have a credible trainer, recruiters may reach out to the student-athlete to determine the top talent in the area. This may help a recruiter build a relationship, or perhaps gain an edge on ways to recruit a student-athlete. Recruiters are not able to be everywhere. Camps in your local area will have writers that cover the event and responsible for blogging or reporting on that event. If a student-athlete does well, they will be recognized as one of the top performers at the event, and may be the featured story. This type of coverage can help recruiters identify some of the top players, and give them a better chance at being recruited. Not all universities have a budget that will allow for their recruiters to be at these events. Instead, these recruiters will rely on the internet and data documented at the event to help them evaluate the student-athlete.

Recruiters also benefit from seeing recruits in person. This is one the reasons that recruiters love one day and summer camps---the student athletes are physically present. This gives them a chance to see if you really are 6′1 and 180 pounds, or 5′8 and 165 pounds. This also allows them to pitch the student-athlete to his head coach and give the recruiter an opportunity to evaluate the student-athlete first-hand. Recruiters often try to get student-athletes and their families to visit the campus "unofficially." Families, be aware that this could be very costly to you, because lots of trips equals lots of money. If several trips are planned, consider visiting schools that are clustered in a defined geographic region (e.g. schools in one state, one part of the country, etc.). This is one way to cut down on the number of trips.

Recruiters often tell student-athletes that if they can get to campus and meet the head coach, then their chances for an offer will increase dramatically. Truthfully, this smacks more of a crafty sales pitch than an honest statement. Do your research before going to any college. If a coaching staff does not make an offer when you visit, then at least you took advantage of the opportunity to visit the campus and gauge whether the coaching staff fits with your student-athlete.

Allan's Scholarship Story

Recruiters need to be effective salesmen, because it is their job to attract the best talent. I have heard many "creative" pitches, as well as numerous scenarios that motivate recruiters to deliver those pitches. Let's look at Allan's story, a manufactured name to protect the privacy of the subject (and university) about whom this story is based.

Allan was one of the top basketball recruits in the state of Florida, and solicited the interest of many scouts from several schools. During the summer Allan would often travel with, and play for his select basketball team, the Florida Heat. While traveling, several top recruiters from New

York wanted Allan to take an unofficial visit and participate in their summer camp that included Syracuse University, St. John's University, and Fordham University, all located in New York State. A persistent recruiter convinced Allan to go to New York and visit Syracuse University. While at Syracuse, Allan participated in their annual basketball camp and had a chance to meet some of the distinguished basketball alumni, tour the facilities, and compete against some of the better basketball players in the Northeast. Allan enjoyed his visit and tweeted on social media about his time at Syracuse University.

Learning of Allan's visit to Syracuse, thanks to the magic of social media, the coaching staff from St. John's and Fordham insisted that Allan and his father make a visit to their campuses. Allan visited both St. John's and Fordham. Fast forward to signing day: Allan did not receive a scholarship offer from Syracuse but was invited to be a preferred walk-on. On national signing day, Allan decided to attend the University of St. John's. During an interview, Allan cited that because he formed a great relationship with the coaching staff, wanted to play basketball in college, and visited the university, he decided to sign with St. John's. Although Allan did not receive a full scholarship offer from Syracuse, the initial reason he went to the state of New York, Allan did receive and sign a national letter of intent because of a camp visit to Syracuse. Lesson? Trust the process.

CHAPTER FIVE

MAKING A LIST

Student-Athlete

Essential to the process is the communication established between the student-athlete and his family. After all, making a decision is not always easy, especially for a young adult who is about to embark on a new chapter in his or her life. And, as with choosing anything, there will be many factors that need to be considered. But patience throughout the process will help get you and your family through it. Here's a thought: At the end of your freshman or sophomore year of high school, write down a list of about 15 schools you want to consider. Now, go through these three factors—factors I believe will help make a decision. This list is not in any particular order, but is intended to provoke you to think more carefully about the journey you are about to take. Thought and value to the journey in making the right decision.

1. **Location:**

Consider Kevin, an all- American recruited by some of the top universities in the nation. Because of Kevin's excellent grades, high SAT score, and athletic achievements, Kevin had scholarship opportunities with the best athletic and academic universities around. Kevin's top 10 list included North Carolina, Purdue, Northwestern, Stanford, Florida, Texas Christian University, Harvard, Notre Dame, Stanford, and Michigan. Kevin is from Texas, and later sat down with his parents to discuss his options. Ultimately, Kevin and his parents determined that location for them was not a factor that mattered and that Kevin had their blessing to attend wherever he wished.

My take: Since Kevin and his family had open minds, I might recommended to them to reconsider location. Because Kevin has lived in Texas his entire life, I might remind them of what they know too well: Blazing heat during much of the year. Here's some more information to guide you a bit in this recommendation of mine: Kevin's parents and lineage are from Jamaica. Because of this, I knew that Kevin is familiar with the southern region of the states, and that his entire family, including Kevin, are quite accustomed to a warmer climate. Therefore, I might suggest that

Kevin give the schools located in the south some points toward his decision, and perhaps reconsider Florida or Texas Christian University? Whatever the choice, location is only one factor, albeit an important one. Kevin accepted a full scholarship from the University of Michigan with a climate on the opposite end of the weather continuum. However, Kevin didn't care much about location. For him, I guess snowy days (and lots of them) are fine. Like Kevin, it is up to you to decide along with your parents. And remember, that means communicating with your parents. Ask yourself if it's important to stay around friends and family? Will the location pose extra stress on your family's finances? Is it important to have easy access to your home (breaks, vacations, and so on)? And what about your family's ability to get to the games to watch you "wow" the crowd? Yep. Lots of things to talk about.

2. **Major/Academics**

At some point during high school, you will need to decide on your major. At 16, I know it is hard to envision what you will be doing at the age of 30, but your major is not a contract for a profession, it is merely a designated area of interest. Still, selecting a major is an essential step in making the right choice. If I wanted to be an actor, I would not go to a college with a poor drama department or to a school without an opportunity to be in school plays. Likewise, it is important to select schools with excellent athletic programs, such as Kansas, Oklahoma State, Oklahoma or Kentucky, to name just a few academics, and fantastic community support.

If I wanted to study engineering, I would want to attend a university with an excellent engineering program. Interested in a business degree? There are many fine universities with exemplary departments of business administration. There are many fine universities that offer superb programs in several disciplines. You will have choices. However, be realistic about how your academics match the admission standards of universities.

For example, if Billy goes to one of the prestigious private secondary schools in the nation, has a 3.8 G.P.A. and scored high on his ACT, then he should consider the top tier academic schools in the nation. **US News and World Report and Forbes Magazine** publishes a list of those top rated colleges and universities every year. Google "Top Colleges and Universities" and a lot of great sites will surface. Look for those that match schools with disciplines (e.g., Best schools with departments in History, Economics, English, and so on.). Don't forget to identify those best schools that are in your home state or town. You may have the very best of both worlds at your doorstep. You will also find that some of the most prestigious colleges and universities are also Division 1: Rice, Tulane, Stanford, Notre Dame, Duke, and Cal-Berkeley, to name just a few. So, you know what? Billy and his family have quite a few choices, and that's a very good thing.

3. **Family Lineage**

I am from Texas and grew up in communities with families that had several generations attend Texas universities. During this time, I often saw two types of cases, the first was Jonathan. His dad was a member of the Texas Longhorns (UT) in the 90's, his uncle graduated from the University of Texas (UT) in 1988, and his cousin attended UT from 2000-2004. His grandfather was a Texas Longhorn from 1963-67, as well as countless other relatives. From the first time I met Jonathan, the only university he ever supported was the University of Texas. He wore Longhorn gear, went to their sporting events, and always talked about going to

UT. Needless to say, the University of Texas was on his list and Jonathan ended up attending The University of Texas to continue the family lineage.

The other case involves Josh. He was a towering 6′7, 260-pound basketball and football player. But unlike Jonathan, Josh did not have any family member who attended a prestigious university. Josh's nearest relatives only attended a local junior college. Josh's only connection to a distinguished university was his little league coach who graduated from Texas A&M University. Josh ended up attending Texas A&M University where he played football and basketball while earning his degree.

In both cases, these two young men had family lineage. In the case of Josh, however, his mentor influenced where he attended. Like location, lineage is a factor, but it is an important one.

Parents

It is important to support the student-athlete as they make such a crucial decision that will affect them the rest of their life. It is important to know that this decision will affect his athletic career, professional career, and maybe who they marry. While there may be many factors going on in the student-athlete's decision making, it is extremely important as a parent to keep their selfishness out of the equation. Some parents try to prostitute their kids to a college, often asking for money, a job, or even housing in exchange for their son/daughter's services. This type of behavior is against the NCAA rules, not to mention the rules of human dignity. As a parent, that sort of behavior should not be unacceptable, but out of the question. Support your child by being a sounding board throughout the journey. If you use selfish motives to motivate your student-athlete, expect nothing but degrading outcomes. Keep your relationship with your child open, honest, and always framed with integrity.

Your job is to assist and manage what is appropriate for your child throughout the recruiting phase. If you do not know how to conduct yourself, ask questions. Ask someone that has been recruited before, or ask the member of a student-athlete's family that has been recruited before. Reach out to coaches that are trustworthy or even past players; they can be extremely helpful. As each of you move forward, eventually visiting universities, ask those in the community what they like and dislike about the university. Ask the players are currently on the team, especially when no one is around to influence what they say, and you will find them to be refreshingly honest.

Parents and Student-Athletes

It is important to sit down and talk about what both parties view as beneficial. Parents and student-athletes will not always see eye to eye. But at the end of the day, it is about supporting the student-athlete with their goals and future. Choosing the wrong university for the wrong reasons is not how you want the athlete to start their adult life. While having a list is an extremely important activity, make sure there is room for open-mindedness about a particular college or university, maybe something that fell off your radar.

Recruiter's Point of View

Recruiters generally recruit in certain areas. Let's take the University of Texas in Austin (UT), for example. Because UT is located in Texas and has a broad scope of players from which to select, the coaching staff may spend most of their efforts in Texas. Certainly there are good players in other states, but Texas is one of those special places that knows football. As a whole understands the importance of high school football, and they have a great feel for their own brand of football.. With Texas being a powerhouse and having endless resources, they will do what is necessary to recruit top athletes. They will go where they need to get what they want, whether it's to Florida, New York, Illinois, California, and well...you get the idea. All the way to Florida, up to New York, over to Illinois, over to Washington, and even hit California. Still, according to rosters, Texas teams are roughly comprised of 80-90 % of its players coming from high schools in Texas.

From a recruiter's point of view, it is usually best to recruit in the area to which you are assigned by the head coach. If a coach played in Mississippi or comes from Mississippi, then he may be the coach responsible for identifying who the best players from Mississippi. Coaches also recruit based upon relationships. Many coaches are former players or have coached for a very long time, which means that they have coached many players who are now high school coaches or played with players who are now high school coaches. A recruiter will reach out to their professional acquaintances to identify who the top players are in that area and if they have a legit shot at recruiting that player.

In general, recruiters recruit players who can play; along with key traits such as good character, good grades, and good attitudes. Academics, lineage, and location play a factor in who, recruits you. Learn how to connect with recruiters by staying alert, staying smart, and staying in shape.

CHAPTER SIX

FINDING THE PERFECT FIT

Student-Athlete

To help find the perfect fit, ask yourself "What am I looking for?" Some universities are located in major cities with huge alumni base, and end up treating their student-athletes like celebrities. If you are fascinated with the glitter and the glory along with the spenders and the stars, then there are types of universities you should consider, namely schools with enormous budgets, traditionally found in larger metropolitan areas such as Miami and Los Angeles.

On the other hand, there are many fine universities located in college towns, typically located near or around larger geographic areas. Examples are Lawrence, Kansas; Lincoln, Nebraska; College Station, Texas; and Norman, Oklahoma. In these towns, students and members of the university community make up most of the town's population. Determine what type of school in what size town is best for you. Determine the environment in which you think you will perform best academically and athletically. When starting this phase of process, you might want to consider three categories of schools: a dream school, a reality school, and a fall back school; instead of a nightmare school, a ridiculous school, and an "Are you kidding me?" school.

A dream school is usually one of the top 10 programs in the country. A reality school is a university that fits your playing ability and generally a place that will show mutual interest, while a fall back school is a place where you can gain admission academically and have the greatest chance to play athletically. Please be realistic. There is nothing worse than listing 10 dream schools and not being recruited by any of those universities.

One of the best ways to find a perfect fit is by visiting the university. Going on an official visit or unofficial visit will help you decide if you can envision yourself there. Going on a visit will give you a better understanding on how big the classroom sizes are, what type of town you will live in, and if you can see yourself playing for that coaching staff. While on your visit, always trust your heart as to where you should go. Although it may go against what others want you to do, pick somewhere that you would want to be for the next 4 or 5 years of your life. There are many universities to consider that are not Division I universities but still offer scholarships. Find what division works for you.

Division I

The most popular division is Division I. This division consists of the power programs like Florida State, UCLA, Tennessee, Michigan State, and Syracuse but also features some smaller institutions like North Texas, Idaho, Troy, Kent State, and Eastern Michigan to name a few. This division is for the most elite prospects and scholarships are usually full ride, so ask the recruiter what type of scholarship they will offer and what it consists of. Every sport is different in the amount of scholarship opportunities they offer. Some schools are Division I in one or two sports and Division II or III in other sports. Do your homework and ask questions. Refer to Appendix C for a list by state.

Division II

The universities are typically smaller public and private universities with under 10,000 students. The scholarships at the

Division II level are equivalency scholarships, which means that the majority of scholarships are partial. You can still get a full scholarship from a Division II school. There is less financial aid available in Division II than Division I. Most athletes are on partial scholarships. Take a look at Appendix D for a list of schools. Although you may not have heard of some of these schools, do your research and inform yourself on the benefits on competing at a particular university. Look at what sports they offer, majors they have, and successful alumni. If your goal is to compete athletically at a university, then please do not look down at a Division II university. While their stadium capacity, financial budget, and sponsorships will not be equivalent to a Division I university, the goal of getting some or all of your education paid for still exists. Concentrate on the size of your dream and not the notoriety of your university. Every year there are players from Division II schools on NFL, NBA and MLB rosters.

Division III

If you are going to compete at a Division III university, the importance of your forty time, bench press, and athletic ability are not weighed as heavily compared to being a Division I prospect.

Division III universities pay close attention to your ACT, SAT, and G.P.A. The amount of aid or scholarship you receive is based upon academic excellence and how much financial aid you qualify for. Division III schools do not have the same budget as a Division I or Division II university, and they recruit athletes who will primarily excel in the classroom as well as on the athletic field. If you are going to attend a Division III school, focus on making the highest ACT/SAT score possible along with a high G.P.A. Please refer to Appendix C for a list of universities.

When finding the perfect fit, keep in mind that every one of your college teammates was once the big man or woman on campus in high school. When you step on that college campus, you start from scratch, needing to prove yourself just as you did in high school. But college is the "Real Deal," and carries with it a no nonsense style. Rest assured your coaches will adopt that same style. You will need to work hard to earn playing time, and as you earn playing time, you have to work twice as hard to keep it. The coaches will recruit players after you that are better than or just as good as you but do not worry. Keep working hard and be the best student-athlete you can be. If this is the place for you, your stars have already been aligned, so just trust the process.

Parents

Finding the perfect fit can be challenging and stressful. One thing to do is to trust the process. As mentioned earlier you should sit down with the student-athlete and come up with three to four schools in the following categories: dream school, reality school, and fall back school. As a parent most of the recruited athletes will go on to attend their fall back school. Parents are usually biased and believe their student-athlete is the best and can compete wherever they want. While having confidence is a plus, every athlete cannot attend a Top 5 or Top 10 program. Sit down with the student-athlete and go over what his or her dream school, reality school, and fall back school would be.

Dream School

Dream schools are usually a Top 10 program. These are the programs most are familiar with in their particular sport as they usually compete on television and have a track record for winning and winning big. An example of a dream school for a men's basketball recruit would be programs such as North Carolina,

Duke, Kentucky, and Kansas. These programs are constantly recruiting the best athletes in the nation and are known as being some of the best programs in the country. Typically a basketball program offers 3 to 5 scholarships a year. So if these four schools are the only schools on his list then there are only 20 athletes in the nation who will be competing at one of these programs. While it may happen, it definitely can be a lofty goal; therefore it should be noted that this would be a dream school.

Reality School

The second category is the *reality school.* A reality school is a place where the student-athlete can fit in both academically and athletically. To help figure out what a reality school is, ask trusted experienced professionals in your circle where the student-athlete's talent would fit. Ask a trainer, coach, or family friend to help state what you think a reality school would be. While figuring out what a reality school is, do your research. If you play quarterback and you are 6'1 and 180 pounds and run a 4.9 in the forty, and every school on your list has a starting quarterback that is 6'4 or taller, then you are taking a risk and that school should not be a reality school. Likewise if the schools on your list have quarterbacks around your height and size, but they all run a forty in 4.5 seconds, then that is not a reality school for your student-athlete. Be realistic in choosing a reality school and make it realistic. This might mean listing smaller Division I programs or even solid Division I-AA and Division II programs.

Fall Back School

A fall back school is a sure thing. Judging by the student-athlete's academic and athletic background, the student-athlete has a high chance of receiving a scholarship. A fall back school is usually a place that shows interest in the student-athlete early or is a university where the student-athlete can definitely excel. Although the term fall back can have negative connotation, a fall back school is usually a good thing. Whether it is a lower tier Division I university or a Division III university, having your tuition paid for is a great accomplishment.

Take Away

Most student-athletes want to attend high profile universities, but weighing the options should always be considered when finding that perfect fit. Remember to consider climate, proximity, coaching staff (coaches change all the time), and academic reputation when making that final decision. If all else fails, go with your gut. Intuition is more powerful than you think.

Recruiter's Point of View

Every off season recruiters and coaching staffs all across the nation sit down and identify needs to help their program. Let's look at a sport like football from a coach's point of view. For the purpose of this example, we will call our fictional university Texas East University. The off-season for Texas East University football begins after signing day in February. The staff at Texas East will all sit down as a staff in a big conference room and begin to identify their needs. They will look at how many seniors are leaving the program, how many underclassmen have left for the NFL draft, how many players have left the program because of academics or suspension, and lastly they will identify players who have season and career-ending injuries. After they identity their needs, they will place a number behind the number of scholarships they will want to distribute for each position. The formula looks like this:

Quarterback(s) – 2 Wide Receiver(s) – 3

Offensive Lineman – 5

Running Back(s) – 0 Tight End(s) - 2 Defensive Lineman – 4

Linebacker(s) – 5 Defensive Back(s) – 3 Punter – 1

Kicker – 0

Total Scholarships - 25

Using this list for guidance, if the student-athlete played running back, this university might not be the best place for him. Do your research, go online, and figure out what the depth chart looks like. Ask your coach how many kids he plans to offer. Understand what players are coming back and what year they are on the playing field. Although this might have been the university you wanted to attend your entire life, a scholarship offer may not be presented if you play running back because they plan to offer zero running backs for the upcoming class. But, if you play offensive line, there is a great chance that you can be one of the players to receive a scholarship as they plan to bring in five offensive lineman this recruiting cycle.

Know this: If you receive a scholarship and the coaching staff offers you early playing time, provided you get that that "A" game going, because there will be intense competition at that position, then get that game going. Never forget that you are leaving a place where you were the best athlete, and now joining a team where your teammates were also the best players on their respective teams. Come in ready to compete and play from day one. And reflect on the importance of being a part of a team. A TEAM!!! Play like you are a part of that team.

CHAPTER SEVEN

SIGNING DAY

Student-Athlete

Signing Day is one of the most rewarding and fun times of your life. There is no greater feeling than signing your name to the university of your choice, while being surrounded and supported by your family, friends, teammates, coaches and school staff.

My signing day story

Signing Day was one of the best days of my life. I had committed to Louisiana Tech about two or three weeks before signing day to play football so my decision on signing day was easy. There was no hat ceremony or surprise switch. All the stress and heaviness from making a decision or choosing a school was gone. I woke up on signing day morning excited about what was to come. As I signed my national letter of intent, I was surrounded by my boys, my teammates, my parents, my loving family, my advisor, and my football coaches. It was a great celebration filled with laughter and cake! One of the best things that happened was listening to my uncle, coaches, and friends give speeches about my hard work and character. I was super excited, and I knew that all my hard work had paid off. But I also knew that in the upcoming months that the real work would begin. As I wrote this I thought: What would a 28 year old tell his 18 year old self? What would a Freshman All American, all conference tight end, who also has his bachelor's degree and master's degree, tell the 18 year old who had just signed his national letter of intent?

I would tell him, if you keep God first, work extremely hard, remain humble, develop relationships with people in the community, and have a spirit of excellence, then you will experience the best four to five years of your life. You will position yourself to be successful on and off the field. You will make memories, travel places, and build friendships with the best people in the world. I would say, go gain as much knowledge as possible, stay true to your core values, and treat everyone with respect. God is always watching! I would tell you to listen to those who came before you, learn from those who are where you are trying to go, and ask questions to those who are where you want to go. Always honor your last name, enjoy the journey, and maintain a spirit of excellence.

Student-athletes, go online and learn when signing day is for you and your prospective sport. Know that if you do not sign on the first day with your peers, do not get discouraged. Coaches will continue to recruit and sign players throughout the time frame to sign a letter of intent. Below is an example of the 2016-2017 Calendar for signing dates.

Signing Dates for Student-Athletes 2016-2017

Sport (s)	Initial Signing Date	Final Signing Date
Basketball (Early Period)	**November 9, 2016**	**November 16, 2016**
Basketball (Regular Period)	**April 12, 2017**	**Division I: May 17, 2017 Division II: August 1, 2017**
Football (Midyear JC Transfer)	**December 14, 2016**	**January 15, 2017**
Football (Regular Period)	**February 1, 2017**	**April 1, 2017**
Soccer and Men's Water Polo	**February 1, 2017**	**August 1, 2017**
All Other Sports (Early Period)	**November 9, 2016**	**November 16, 2016**
All Other Sports (Regular Period)	**April 12, 2017**	**August 1, 2017**

Junior College Option 1 (Academic Qualifier)

If you do not sign a scholarship offer on signing day, do not get discouraged. There are other options out there to continue your education and athletic career. The first option is to attend a junior college. If you qualify academically, meaning that you have registered with the NCAA Eligibility Center, then the requirements to transfer to a 4 year university are:

- Achieve a cumulative G.P.A of 2.0
- Complete at least 12 transferable credit hours
- Attend the junior college for at least one semester or quarter.
- If you play basketball or baseball you may not transfer during the middle of the year and play that same year.

Junior College Option 2 (Non Qualifier)

To transfer from a junior college to a 4-year university you must attend the two-year college full time for at least three semesters or four quarters, have a cumulative G.P.A of 2.0., graduate from the two-year college (JuCo) with your associate degree or have 48 transferable credit hours at a semester school and 72 transferable credit hours at a quarter school.

If you are not sure what your transfer status is or what your options are with a junior college, meet with your academic counselor or advisor to gain a greater understanding. Also sit down with your parents and research online what your options are to transfer from the junior college if you decide to attend.

Preparatory Academy Option 3

For many basketball players, attending a preparatory academy after high school is commonplace. A preparatory academy is essentially a 5th year of high school and will give recruits another year to work on their game and potentially attract an offer from a university. If your grades are not strong enough to attend a university, then a preparatory academy is not an option. To learn more about preparatory academies go online and research some options.

Parents

The thought of your student-athlete leaving home and going several hundred miles away is not always the most desirable feeling. But seeing your son or daughter fulfill a dream is worth all the late night games, morning drop offs, weekend games, and other sacrifices you have made over the years. This is definitely a time of celebration for both the parents and student-athletes. Usually your local high school will have a signing day ceremony on national signing day. Coordinate with your head coach or academic counselor to know the date, time, and location. Make sure you invite close family and friends that have impacted the student-athlete on their journey. It is great when a community comes together to celebrate the student-athlete. While signing the student-athlete's name on signing day is the goal, everyone will not achieve that. If you and your student-athlete are in that bucket, do not worry. University coaches are still looking for talent. Encourage the student-athlete to stay in shape, stay working out, and make sure their ACT/SAT score is as high as it can be.

Shortly after signing day, there are many states that host a *"showcase event"*. This showcase is aimed at giving Division II and Division III schools an opportunity to recruit some of the student-athletes that did not sign on national signing day. These events are usually free, but may be around $30 to participate in. Student-athletes are asked to pre-register, with their G.P.A and ACT/SAT score being two of the things coaches will be looking for. Upon registering, the student-athletes will go through a combined workout in front of 30 to 50 scouts with the hope of finding some talented student-athletes. If your athlete has some talent and has taken care of business in the classroom, there is a spot for him or her. Once you student-athlete decides on a university, have a celebration or signing day party to celebrate the accomplishment.

Recruiter's Point of View

Signing Day is one of the most rewarding days for a recruiter. Many recruiters have spent two or three years forming a relationship with student-athletes and their family. To have a student-athlete sign a national letter of intent to their university is the goal. As a coaching staff, the recruiters meet in a team meeting room waiting for the national letters of intent to be submitted. As they come in, the coaching staffs celebrate the rewards of their hard work. There are surprises that occur. One student-athlete may be committed to one university and then decides to change on signing day. Some recruits have not decided and signing day is their chance to make a decision. This can be disappointing to some coaches, but most recruit multiple players at a position to make sure that they are not putting all their eggs in one basket.

After signing day the work does not stop, as recruiters will meet to make sure all the needs are met for that particular class. If there are needs that were not addressed, the coaches will continue to look for talent at that position. Some coaches will attend showcases, while other coaches will make calls to connections to fill their need. Nevertheless, a recruiter's job is never done; the coaching staff will begin formulating relationships with the next crop of athletes and their families.

APPENDIX A

Cover Letter Example

July 28, 2018

John Doe
Northwestern University Football
1501 Central Street
Evanston, IL 60208

Dear Coach Doe,

I appreciate your taking the time to review the questionnaire I submitted and viewing my highlights.

I know that you are looking for a well-rounded student-athlete, and I wanted to briefly share with you my academic resume. I have also attached my most recent ACT scores and transcripts. I am interested in playing football for Northwestern University.

I look forward to hearing from you. Again, thank you for your time and consideration.

Sincerely,

Anthony D. Harrison

APPENDIX B

Resume Example

Anthony D. Harrison 6'4 230 4.5 Class of 2020
anthonydrewharrison@gmail.com
777 Preston Houston, Texas 77002
(832)555-5505
http://www.hudl.com/athlete/5555455/anthony-harrison

EDUCATION
Oak Grove School
3500 Smiley Dr.
Houston, TX 77036
(713)555-7651

Academic Counselor
Mrs. Ashley Thornton
713-555-5515
ashley_thornton@gmail.com

Head Football Coach
Mr. Tony Harrison
713-555-5555
TonydrewHarrison@gmail.com

ACTIVITIES

National Honor Society	Present
Boys and Girls Club	2016-2018
High School Varsity Football	2016-2018
High School Varsity Basketball	2016-2018

HONORS
- National Honor Society
- Honorable Mention All-State
- Academic All-District Team

COMMUNITY SERVICE
- Boys and Girls Club
- Houston Food Bank

APPENDIX C

Alabama
University of Alabama
Alabama A&M University
Alabama State University
University of Alabama at Birmingham
Auburn University
Jacksonville State University
Samford University
University of South Alabama
Troy University

Arkansas
Arkansas State University
University of Arkansas, Fayetteville
University of Arkansas at Little Rock
University of Arkansas, Pine Bluff
University of Central Arkansas

Arizona
University of Arizona
Arizona State University
Grand Canyon University
Northern Arizona University

California
California Polytechnic State University
California State University, Bakersfield
California State University, Fresno
California State University, Fullerton
California State University, Northridge
California State University, Sacramento
University of California, Berkeley
University of California, Davis
University of California, Irvine
University of California, Los Angeles
University of California, Riverside
University of California, Santa Barbara
Long Beach State University
Loyola Marymount University
University of the Pacific

Pepperdine University
University of San Diego
San Diego State University
University of San Francisco
San Jose State University
Santa Clara University
University of Southern California
St. Mary's College of California
Stanford University

Colorado
University of Colorado, Boulder
Colorado State University
University of Denver
University of Northern Colorado
U.S. Air Force Academy

Connecticut
Central Connecticut State University
University of Connecticut
Fairfield University
Quinnipiac University
Sacred Heart University
Yale University

District of Columbia
American University
George Washington University
Georgetown University
Howard University

Delaware
University of Delaware
Delaware State University

Florida
Bethune-Cookman University
University of Central Florida
University of Florida
Florida A&M University
Florida Atlantic University
Florida Gulf Coast University
Florida International University

Florida State University
Jacksonville University
University of Miami (Florida)
University of North Florida
University of South Florida
Stetson University

Georgia
University of Georgia
Georgia Institute of Technology
Georgia Southern University
Georgia State University
Kennesaw State University
Mercer University
Savannah State University

Hawaii
University of Hawaii, Manoa

Iowa
Drake University
University of Iowa
Iowa State University
University of Northern Iowa

Idaho
Boise State University
University of Idaho
Idaho State University

Illinois
Bradley University
Chicago State University
DePaul University
Eastern Illinois University
Illinois State University
University of Illinois Urbana-Champaign
University of Illinois at Chicago
Loyola University Chicago
Northern Illinois University
Northwestern University
Southern Illinois University at Carbondale

Southern Illinois University Edwardsville
Western Illinois University

Indiana
Ball State University
Butler University
University of Evansville
Indiana State University
Indiana University, Bloomington
Indiana University-Purdue University, Fort Wayne
Indiana University-Purdue University at Indianapolis
University of Notre Dame
Purdue University
Valparaiso University

Kansas
University of Kansas
Kansas State University
Wichita State University

Kentucky
Eastern Kentucky University
University of Kentucky
University of Louisville
Morehead State University
Murray State University
Northern Kentucky University
Western Kentucky University

Louisiana
Grambling State University
University of Louisiana at Lafayette
University of Louisiana at Monroe
Louisiana State University
Louisiana Tech University
McNeese State University
University of New Orleans
Nicholls State University
Northwestern State University
Southeastern Louisiana University
Southern University, Baton Rouge

Tulane University

Massachusetts
Boston College
Boston University
Harvard University
College of the Holy Cross
University of Massachusetts, Amherst
University of Massachusetts Lowell
Northeastern University

Maryland
Coppin State University
Loyola University Maryland
University of Maryland Eastern Shore
University of Maryland, Baltimore County
University of Maryland, College Park
Morgan State University
Mount St. Mary's University
Towson University
U.S. Naval Academy

Maine
University of Maine, Orono

Michigan
Central Michigan University
University of Detroit Mercy
Eastern Michigan University
University of Michigan
Michigan State University
Oakland University
Western Michigan University

Minnesota
University of Minnesota, Twin Cities

Missouri
Missouri State University
University of Missouri, Columbia
University of Missouri-Kansas City
Southeast Missouri State University
Saint Louis University

Mississippi
Alcorn State University
Jackson State University
University of Mississippi
Mississippi State University
Mississippi Valley State University
The University of Southern Mississippi

Montana
University of Montana
Montana State University-Bozeman

North Carolina
Appalachian State University
Campbell University
Davidson College
Duke University
East Carolina University
Elon University
Gardner-Webb University
High Point University
University of North Carolina-Asheville
North Carolina A&T State University
North Carolina Central University
North Carolina State University
University of North Carolina Wilmington
University of North Carolina, Chapel Hill
The University of North Carolina at Charlotte
The University of North Carolina at Greensboro
Wake Forest University
Western Carolina University

North Dakota
University of North Dakota
North Dakota State University

Nebraska
Creighton University
University of Nebraska Omaha
University of Nebraska, Lincoln

New Hampshire
Dartmouth College
University of New Hampshire

New Jersey
Fairleigh Dickinson University, Metropolitan Campus
Monmouth University
New Jersey Institute of Technology
Princeton University
Rider University
Rutgers, The State University of New Jersey, New Brunswick
Seton Hall University
Saint Peter's University

New Mexico
University of New Mexico
New Mexico State University

Nevada
University of Nevada, Las Vegas
University of Nevada, Reno

New York
University at Albany
Binghamton University
University at Buffalo, the State University of New York
Colgate University
Columbia University-Barnard College
Cornell University
Fordham University
Hofstra University
Iona College
Long Island University-Brooklyn Campus
Manhattan College
Marist College
Niagara University
Siena College
St. Bonaventure University
St. Francis College Brooklyn
St. John's University (New York)
Stony Brook University
Syracuse University
U.S. Military Academy

Wagner College

Ohio
University of Akron
Bowling Green State University
University of Cincinnati
Cleveland State University
University of Dayton
Kent State University
Miami University (Ohio)
The Ohio State University
Ohio University
University of Toledo
Wright State University
Xavier University
Youngstown State University

Oklahoma
University of Oklahoma
Oklahoma State University
Oral Roberts University
The University of Tulsa

Oregon
University of Oregon
Oregon State University
University of Portland
Portland State University

Pennsylvania
Bucknell University
Drexel University
Duquesne University
La Salle University
Lafayette College
Lehigh University
University of Pennsylvania
Pennsylvania State University
University of Pittsburgh
Robert Morris University
Saint Francis University (Pennsylvania)
Saint Joseph's University

Temple University
Villanova University

Rhode Island
Brown University
Bryant University
Providence College
University of Rhode Island

South Carolina
College of Charleston (South Carolina)
Charleston Southern University
The Citadel
Clemson University
Coastal Carolina University
Furman University
Presbyterian College
University of South Carolina, Columbia
South Carolina State University
University of South Carolina Upstate
Winthrop University
Wofford College

South Dakota
University of South Dakota
South Dakota State University

Tennessee
Austin Peay State University
Belmont University
East Tennessee State University
Lipscomb University
University of Memphis
Middle Tennessee State University
Tennessee State University
Tennessee Technological University
University of Tennessee at Chattanooga
University of Tennessee, Knoxville
University of Tennessee at Martin
Vanderbilt University

Texas
Abilene Christian University
Baylor University
University of Houston
Houston Baptist University
University of the Incarnate Word
Lamar University
University of North Texas
Prairie View A&M University
Rice University
Sam Houston State University
Southern Methodist University
Stephen F. Austin State University
Texas A&M University, College Station
Texas A&M University-Corpus Christi
Texas Christian University
The University of Texas Rio Grande Valley
Texas Southern University
Texas State University
Texas Tech University
University of Texas at Arlington
University of Texas at Austin
University of Texas at El Paso
University of Texas at San Antonio

Utah
Brigham Young University
Southern Utah University
University of Utah
Utah State University
Utah Valley University
Weber State University

Virginia
George Mason University
Hampton University
James Madison University
Liberty University
Longwood University
Norfolk State University
Old Dominion University
Radford University

University of Richmond
University of Virginia
Virginia Commonwealth University
Virginia Military Institute
Virginia Polytechnic Institute and State University
College of William and Mary

Vermont
University of Vermont

Washington
Eastern Washington University
Gonzaga University
Seattle University
University of Washington
Washington State University

Wisconsin
Marquette University
University of Wisconsin-Green Bay
University of Wisconsin, Madison
University of Wisconsin, Milwaukee

West Virginia
Marshall University
West Virginia University

Wyoming
University of Wyoming

Appendix D

Alaska
University of Alaska Anchorage
University of Alaska Fairbanks

Alabama
University of Alabama in Huntsville
Miles College
University of Montevallo
University of North Alabama
Spring Hill College
Stillman College
Tuskegee University
University of West Alabama

Arkansas
Arkansas Tech University
University of Arkansas, Fort Smith
University of Arkansas, Monticello
Harding University
Henderson State University
Ouachita Baptist University
Southern Arkansas University

Arizona
Grand Canyon University

British Columbia
Simon Fraser University

California
Academy of Art University
Azusa Pacific University
California Baptist University
California State Polytechnic University, Pomona
California State University, Monterey Bay
California State University, Chico
California State University, Dominguez Hills
California State University, East Bay

California State University, Los Angeles
California State University, San Bernardino
California State University, Stanislaus
California State University, San Marcos
University of California, San Diego
Concordia University Irvine
Dominican University of California
Fresno Pacific University
Holy Names University
Humboldt State University
Notre Dame de Namur University
Point Loma Nazarene University
San Francisco State University
Sonoma State University

Colorado
Adams State University
Colorado Christian University
Colorado Mesa University
Colorado School of Mines
Colorado State University-Pueblo
University of Colorado, Colorado Springs
Fort Lewis College
Metropolitan State University of Denver
Regis University (Colorado)
Western State Colorado University

Connecticut
University of Bridgeport
University of New Haven
Post University
Southern Connecticut State University

District of Columbia
University of the District of Columbia

Delaware
Goldey-Beacom College
Wilmington University (Delaware)

Florida
Barry University

Eckerd College
Embry-Riddle Aeronautical University (Florida)
Flagler College
Florida Institute of Technology
Florida Southern College
Lynn University
Nova Southeastern University
Palm Beach Atlantic University
Rollins College
Saint Leo University
University of Tampa
University of West Florida

Georgia
Albany State University (Georgia)
Armstrong State University
Clark Atlanta University
Clayton State University
Columbus State University
Emmanuel College (Georgia)
Fort Valley State University
Georgia College
Georgia Regents University
Georgia Southwestern State University
Morehouse College
University of North Georgia
Paine College
Shorter University
Valdosta State University
University of West Georgia
Young Harris College

Hawaii
Brigham Young University, Hawaii
Chaminade University
University of Hawaii at Hilo
Hawaii Pacific University

Iowa
Upper Iowa University

Idaho
Northwest Nazarene University

Illinois
University of Illinois at Springfield
Lewis University
McKendree University
Quincy University

Indiana
University of Indianapolis
Oakland City University
University of Southern Indiana
Saint Joseph's College (Indiana)

Kansas
Emporia State University
Fort Hays State University
Newman University
Pittsburg State University
Washburn University of Topeka

Kentucky
Bellarmine University
Kentucky State University
Kentucky Wesleyan College
Northern Kentucky University

Massachusetts
American International College
Assumption College
Bentley University
University of Massachusetts Lowell
Merrimack College
Stonehill College

Maryland
Bowie State University

Michigan
Ferris State University
Grand Valley State University
Hillsdale College
Lake Superior State University
Michigan Technological University

Northern Michigan University
Northwood University (Michigan)
Saginaw Valley State University
Wayne State University (Michigan)

Minnesota
Bemidji State University
Concordia University, St. Paul
Minnesota State University, Mankato
Minnesota State University, Moorhead
University of Minnesota, Crookston
University of Minnesota Duluth
Southwest Minnesota State University
St. Cloud State University
Winona State University

Missouri
University of Central Missouri
Drury University
Lincoln University (Missouri)
Lindenwood University
Maryville University of Saint Louis
Missouri University of Science and Technology
Missouri Southern State University
Missouri Western State University
University of Missouri-St. Louis
Northwest Missouri State University
Rockhurst University
Southwest Baptist University
Truman State University
William Jewell College

Mississippi
Delta State University
Mississippi College

Montana
Montana State University Billings

North Carolina
Barton College
Belmont Abbey College
Brevard College

Catawba College
Chowan University
Elizabeth City State University
Fayetteville State University
Johnson C. Smith University
Lees-McRae College
Lenoir-Rhyne University
Livingstone College
Mars Hill University
University of Mount Olive
University of North Carolina at Pembroke
Pfeiffer University
Queens University of Charlotte
Shaw University
Saint Augustine's University
Wingate University
Winston-Salem State University

North Dakota
University of Mary
Minot State University

Nebraska
Chadron State College
University of Nebraska Omaha
University of Nebraska at Kearney
Wayne State College (Nebraska)

New Hampshire
Franklin Pierce University
Southern New Hampshire University
Saint Anselm College

New Jersey
Bloomfield College
Caldwell University
Felician College
Georgian Court University

New Mexico
Eastern New Mexico University
New Mexico Highlands University
Western New Mexico University

New York
Adelphi University
Concordia College (New York)
Daemen College
Dominican College (New York)
Dowling College
Le Moyne College
Mercy College
Molloy College
New York Institute of Technology
Nyack College
Pace University
Long Island University/LIU Post
Queens College (New York)
Robert Wesleyan College
The College of St. Rose
St. Thomas Aquinas College

Ohio
Ashland University
Cedarville University
Central State University
University of Findlay
Lake Erie College
Malone University
Notre Dame College (Ohio)
Ohio Dominican University
Tiffin University
Urbana University
Ursuline College
Walsh University

Oklahoma
Cameron University
University of Central Oklahoma
East Central University
Northeastern State University
Northwestern Oklahoma State University
Oklahoma Baptist University
Oklahoma Christian University
Oklahoma Panhandle State University
Rogers State University

Southeastern Oklahoma State University
Southern Nazarene University
Southwestern Oklahoma State University

Oregon
Concordia University Portland
Western Oregon University

Pennsylvania
Bloomsburg University of Pennsylvania
California University of Pennsylvania
Chestnut Hill College
Cheyney University of Pennsylvania
Clarion University of Pennsylvania
East Stroudsburg University of Pennsylvania
Edinboro University of Pennsylvania
Gannon University
Holy Family University
Indiana University of Pennsylvania
Kutztown University of Pennsylvania
The Lincoln University (Pennsylvania)
Lock Haven University of Pennsylvania
Mansfield University of Pennsylvania
Mercyhurst University
Millersville University of Pennsylvania
Philadelphia University
University of Pittsburgh, Johnstown
University of the Sciences in Philadelphia
Seton Hill University
Shippensburg University of Pennsylvania
Slippery Rock University of Pennsylvania
West Chester University of Pennsylvania

Puerto Rico
University of Puerto Rico, Bayamon
University of Puerto Rico, Mayaguez
University of Puerto Rico, Rio Piedras

South Carolina
Anderson University (South Carolina)
Benedict College
Claflin University
Coker College

Converse College
Erskine College
Francis Marion University
Lander University
Limestone College
Newberry College
North Greenville University
University of South Carolina Aiken
Southern Wesleyan University

South Dakota
Augustana College (South Dakota)
Black Hills State University
Northern State University
University of Sioux Falls
South Dakota School of Mines & Technology

Tennessee
Carson-Newman University
Christian Brothers University
King University
Lane College
Lee University
LeMoyne-Owen College
Lincoln Memorial University
Trevecca Nazarene University
Tusculum College
Union University

Texas
Abilene Christian University
Angelo State University
Dallas Baptist University
University of the Incarnate Word
Lubbock Christian University
Midwestern State University
St. Edward's University
St. Mary's University (Texas)
Tarleton State University
Texas A&M International University
Texas A&M University-Commerce
Texas A&M University-Kingsville
University of Texas of the Permian Basin

Texas Woman's University
West Texas A&M University

Utah
Dixie State University

Virginia
The University of Virginia's College at Wise
Virginia State University
Virginia Union University
Saint Michael's College

Washington
Central Washington University
Seattle Pacific University
Saint Martin's University
Western Washington University
Wisconsin
University of Wisconsin, Parkside

West Virginia
Alderson Broaddus University
Bluefield State College
University of Charleston (West Virginia)
Concord University
Davis and Elkins College
Fairmont State University
Glenville State College
Ohio Valley University
Salem International University
Shepherd University
West Liberty University
West Virginia State University
West Virginia Wesleyan College
Wheeling Jesuit University

CONTACT THE AUTHOR

Connect on Social Media at:

Instagram @AnthonyDrewHarrison

Twitter @The_Top_Recruit

Facebook @ Anthony Drew Harrison (A-Train)

Visit www.thetoprecruit.org for more information on booking & appearances.

Email: info@mcdowellsbrandinggroup.com for interview and speaking request.

Made in the USA
San Bernardino, CA
06 May 2017